T0197379

When Butterflies Fly

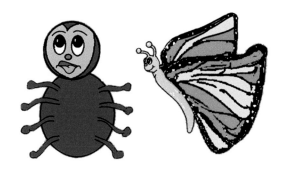

Regina Dahl

WestBow Press books may be ordered through booksellers or by contacting:

WestBow Press
A Division of Thomas Nelson & Zondervan
1663 Liberty Drive
Bloomington, IN 47403
www.westbowpress.com
844-714-3454

Because of the dynamic nature of the Internet, any web addresses or links contained in this book may have changed since publication and may no longer be valid. The views expressed in this work are solely those of the author and do not necessarily reflect the views of the publisher, and the publisher hereby disclaims any responsibility for them.

Any people depicted in stock imagery provided by Getty Images are models, and such images are being used for illustrative purposes only. Certain stock imagery © Getty Images.

ISBN: 978-1-4497-8095-1 (sc)
ISBN: 978-1-4497-8096-8 (e)

Library of Congress Control Number: 2012924256

Print information available on the last page.

WestBow Press rev. date: 08/23/2022

One day, in a small garden, a beautiful butterfly met a busy spider that was spinning a web.

The butterfly soon found out that the spider loved to talk, but would sometimes become a little bit pushy and bossy. As they visited, the butterfly became uncomfortable.

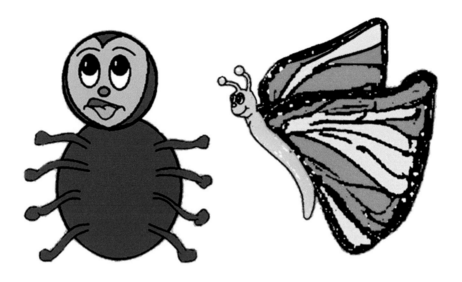

The spider seemed happy as long as they always did what the spider wanted to do. Whenever the butterfly said something, or suggested they do anything, the spider was simply not interested, and responded with, "Oh, what would you know? You are just a butterfly."

"Your wings are really too big." said the spider. "Here, let me help you. Have you ever thought about wearing a different color, perhaps?"

Knowing that God created everyone special, the butterfly ignored the spider's silly comments and continued to bless the spider.

"What a lovely home you have," said the butterfly.

"Yes, I know," said the spider proudly. "Let me show you the best part. I have the grandest shoe collection in the entire garden."

As they went toward the shoe room, the spider said, "You are not like my other friends. My other friends are happy to do whatever I want them to. You seem very unhappy. If you do not enjoy the way that I treat you, then I think you have a problem. What you need is to be more like my friends and me, and I can help you." Then, the spider added, "By the way, you should really practice flying more. You are not very good at it."

With that, the spider opened the door to the shoe room.

"Oh, this is very nice," the butterfly said kindly.

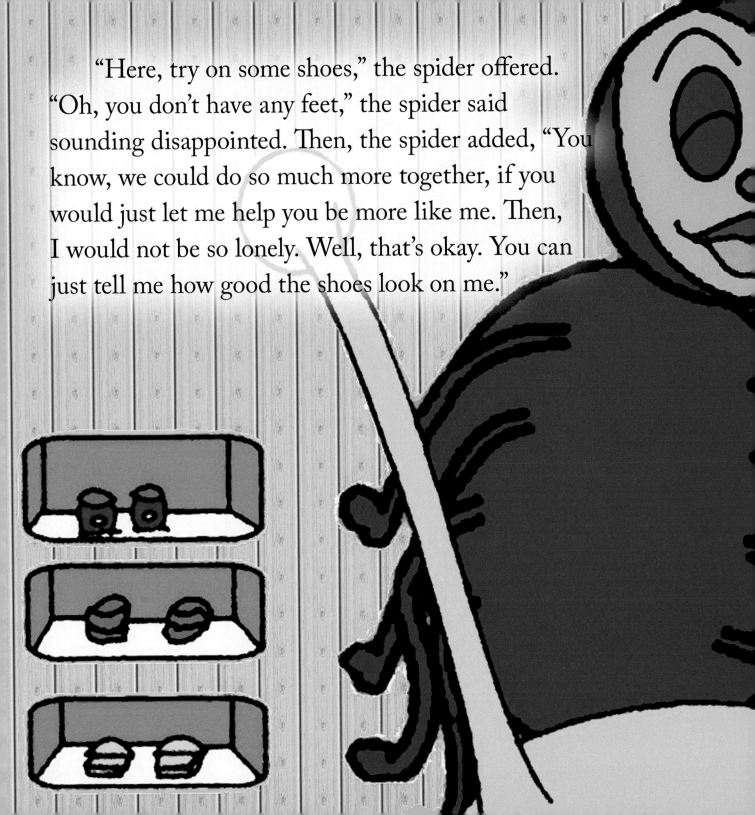

"Here, try on some shoes," the spider offered. "Oh, you don't have any feet," the spider said sounding disappointed. Then, the spider added, "You know, we could do so much more together, if you would just let me help you be more like me. Then, I would not be so lonely. Well, that's okay. You can just tell me how good the shoes look on me."

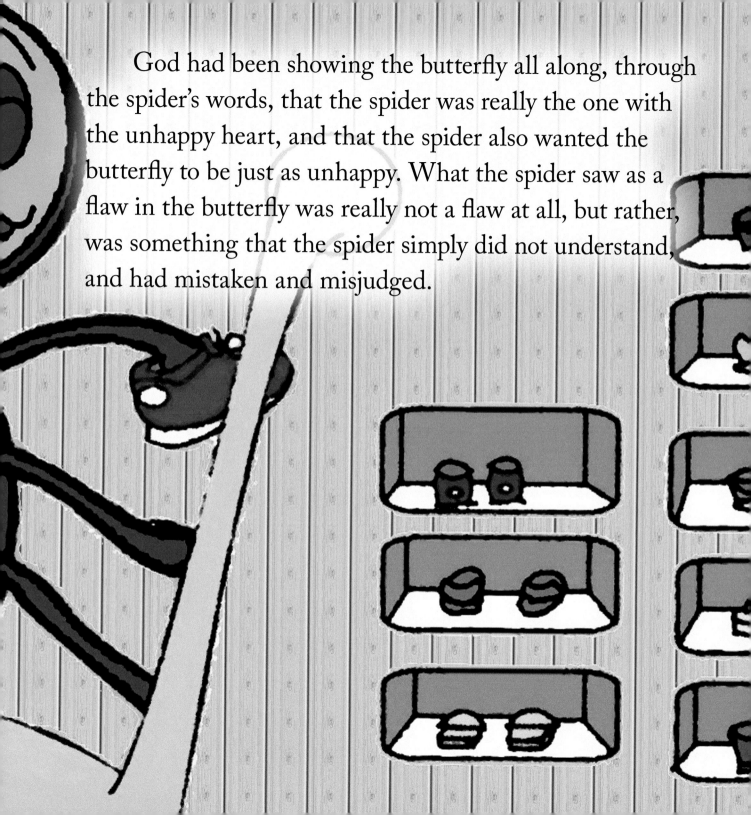

God had been showing the butterfly all along, through the spider's words, that the spider was really the one with the unhappy heart, and that the spider also wanted the butterfly to be just as unhappy. What the spider saw as a flaw in the butterfly was really not a flaw at all, but rather, was something that the spider simply did not understand, and had mistaken and misjudged.

That night, the butterfly simply
said a prayer for the spider.

Deep down, the spider did not like itself and wanted to change, but it did not know how. The spider noticed that the butterfly was happy and friendly, and was always giving and kind to others.

How can I be more like the butterfly? The spider wondered.

After trying everything, including a pair of wings, it did not take the spider long to find out that nothing that the spider did on its own could make it more like the butterfly.

Then, the spider realized that maybe just being honest with God would be best. God already knew and loved the spider completely and perfectly just the way it was. God just wanted to heal the spider so that it could be free. Then, the spider could truly love others.

So, the spider told God everything, chose to forgive, began thinking about what God said about the spider, and was healed by God's Love. Then, the spider no longer felt like trying to put others down to feel important. The spider was already important to God. Also, just knowing that God was with the spider caused the spider to not be lonely. Therefore, the spider did not feel the need to behave selfishly with others anymore. Because God loved the spider, the spider could also love itself.

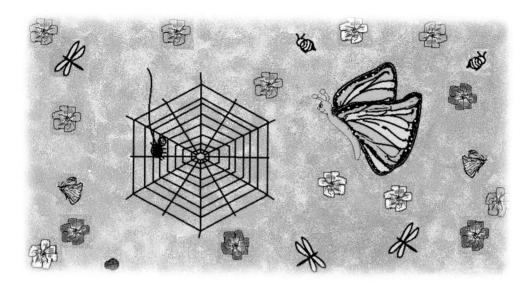

As the spider believed God, it was more loving and became better friends with the other bugs and butterflies in the garden.

Printed in the United States
by Baker & Taylor Publisher Services